**DEDICATED TO
LINDSAY DALTON MALLERS**
FOR LIVING THE QUESTIONS

AND TO JULIET & PHOEBE
FOR THEIR INTUITIVE HEARTS

**ANCIENT GREEKS BELIEVED BEES WERE THE EMBODIMENT OF THE GODDESS OF APHRODITE:
THE GODDESS OF LOVE**

**Welcome to our hive! It's over in that tree
It really is Alive...Come on over you can see**

**We chose this special spot with many flowers growing 'round
Your Home is where you thrive...What grows brightest in your ground?**

We're only here on Earth for 5-6 whole weeks. Except for our sweet queen she's busy loving like a bee! She gets 4 years to guide us and teach us all with love. How would you spend your life if you had the time above?

There are endless possibilities and ways to spend our time
these are some ideas to make our lives sublime

**Just like colors of the rainbow our missions complement each other
Each and every One is valued so we can all grow stronger**

Some bees brave the elements to forage for our food. They can get a little scared out in the Great Big World. When you yourself feel fear, what helps you carry on? What do you say to calm your mind and get back to your heart?

each bee makes about 1/10th teaspoon of honey in their lifetime

**For just one pound of honey, we need 2 million flowers
Every tiny droplet helps: We each have useful powers**

honey has been known as the elixir of life for centuries

With lots of work to do, it somehow still gets done. We have spare honey to share (with you!) and time to have some fun. What do you like to share? What do you have the most of? What would you like to give the world a little extra dose of?

Without our Mother Earth we couldn't do one bit
She shares forever with us all
To give back: we cannot quit.

**For us bees we love her most for growing lots of flowers
What would you give Earth most thanks for? (Be sure to go and tell her!)**

anther: the part of the flower that contains pollen

We call this love abundance... It's truly quite the dance
We hop around and skip and fly, from anther to anther we prance

You can see all of our joy when we get back to our hive
We have a DANCE PARTY to celebrate our strides

Our dance is called the Waggle: we wiggle back and forth
It guides family to the flowers with the help of their True North

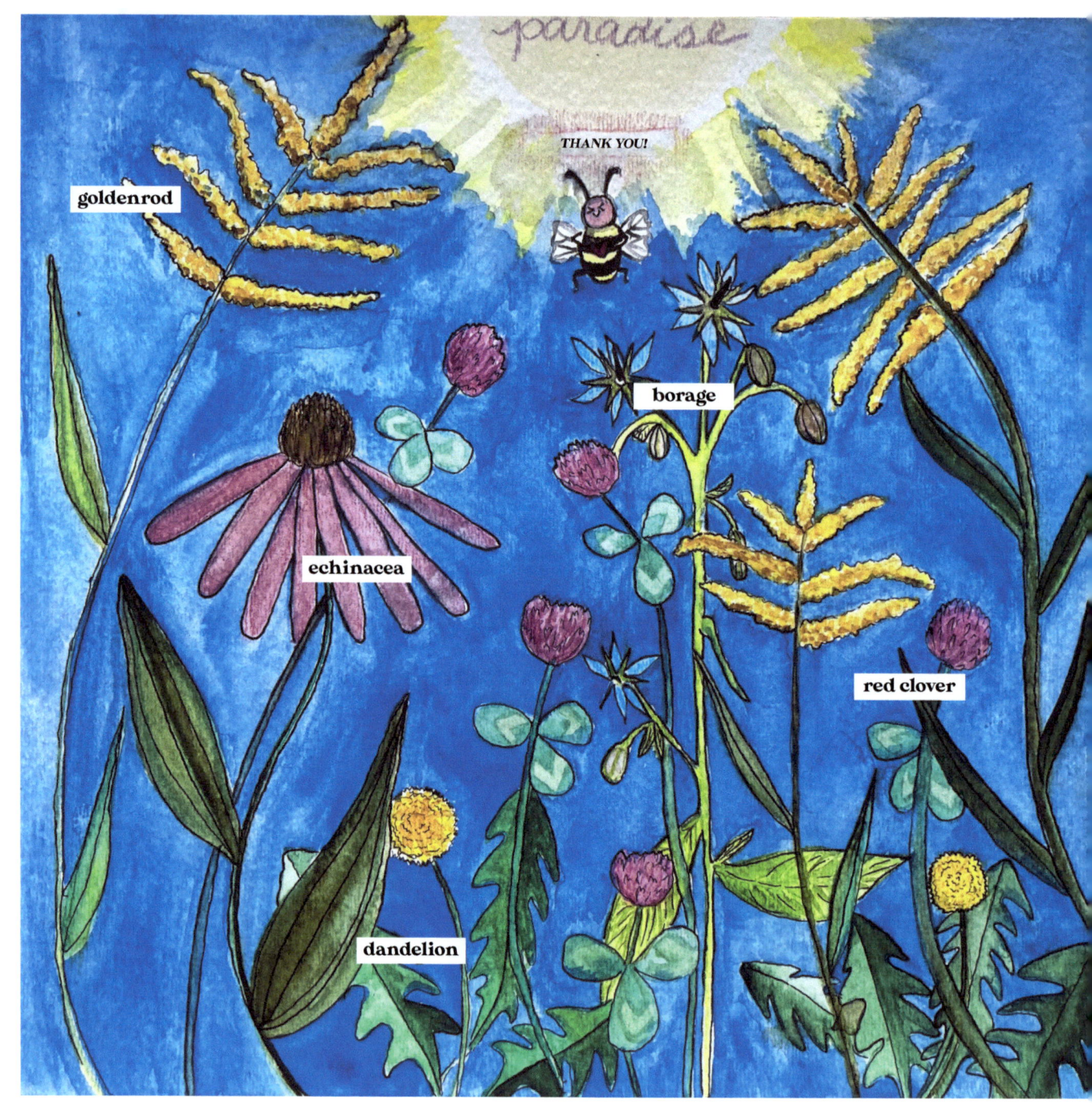

**We really have a lot of fun just being a sweet bee
How will you enjoy your time while you're a human being?**

**The greatest hope we have is that all are Loved and Free
What will You do today to Love more like a bee?**

The face of our bee friend was inpsired by the most loving face of my dear friend Lindsay. May we all smile upon those we love.

www.ingramcontent.com/pod-product-compliance
Lightning Source LLC
Chambersburg PA
CBHW041408160426
42811CB00106B/1556